D1741743

# SPIDER-MAN™

## THE VISUAL GUIDE TO THE COMPLETE MOVIE TRILOGY

# STUNG BY FATE

# DK

LONDON, NEW YORK,
MELBOURNE, MUNICH AND DELHI

**Project Editor**  Laura Gilbert
**Designer**  Lynne Moulding
**Publishing Manager**  Simon Beecroft
**Brand Manager**  Lisa Lanzarini
**Category Publisher**  Alex Allan
**Production Controller**  Nick Seston
**DTP Designer**  Hanna Ländin

First published in Great Britain in 2007 by
Dorling Kindersley Limited,
80 Strand, London, WC2R 0RL
A Penguin Company

Spider-Man and all related characters: TM & © 2007 Marvel Characters, Inc.
Spider-Man, the movie: © 2007 Columbia Pictures Industries, Industries, Inc.
All rights reserved.

Page design copyright © 2007 Dorling Kindersley Limited
A Penguin Company

2 4 6 8 10 9 7 5 3 1
SD283 – 01/07

All rights reserved. No part of this publication may be reproduced, stored in
a retrieval system, or transmitted in any form or by any means, electronic,
mechanical, photocopying, recording, or otherwise, without the prior
written permission of the copyright owner.

A CIP catalogue record for this book is
available from the British Library

ISBN: 978-1-40532-011-5

Printed and bound by Leo Paper Products Ltd., China
Colour development by MDP, UK

Discover more at
www.dk.com

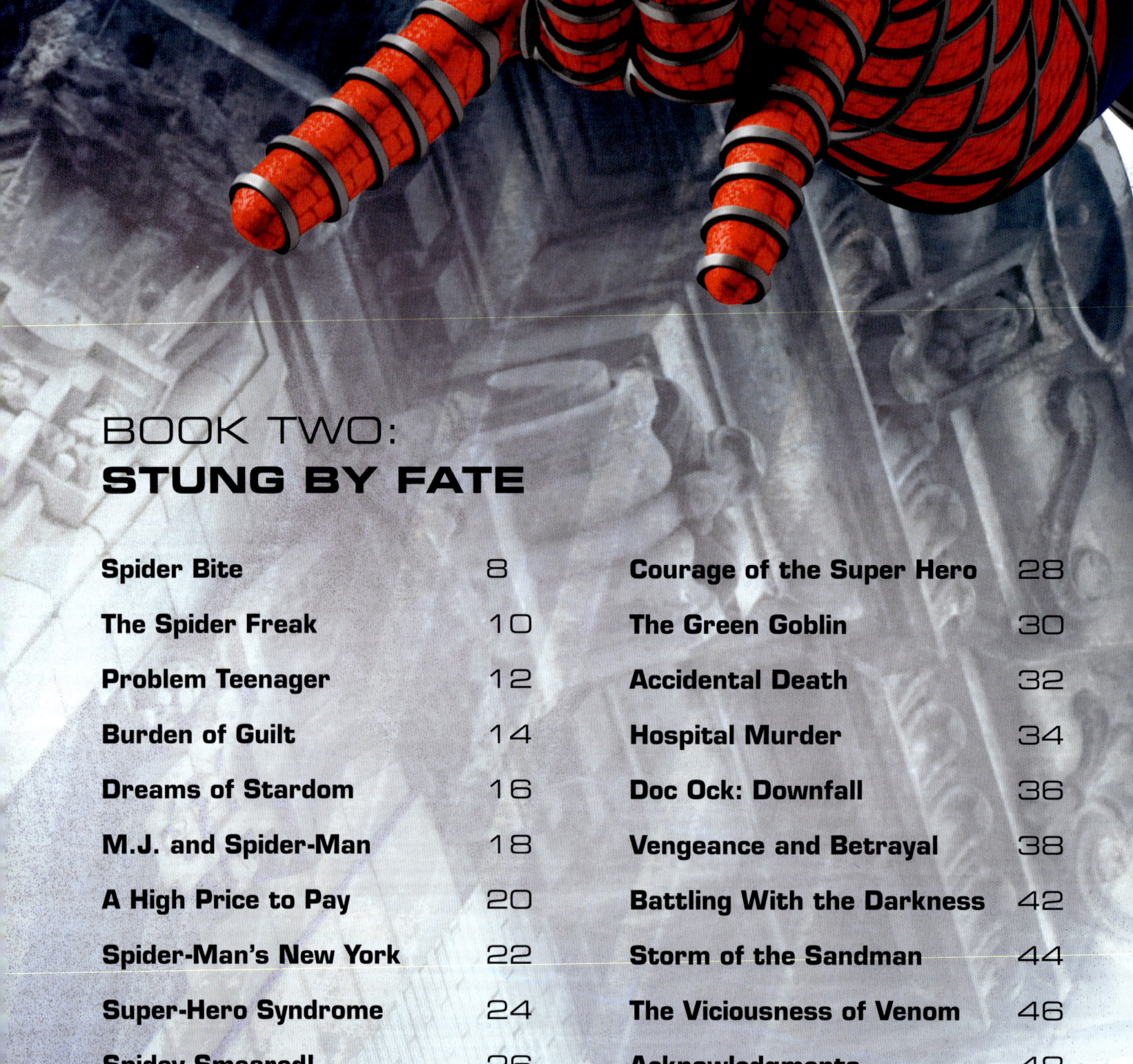

# BOOK TWO:
# STUNG BY FATE

**"** She looks at me every day. Mary Jane Watson. Oh, boy. If she only knew how I felt about her. But she can never know. **"**

# SPIDER
# BITE

Peter Parker's high-school class was on a field trip to Columbia University's science department. Ground-breaking genetic research was being carried out there into certain species of arachnids—spiders. Peter was keen to record the visit by taking some photos for the school paper. Maybe he would get a chance to get M.J. in the picture, too, he thought. But as he took the shot he felt a sudden, sharp pain in his hand...

**Keeping order** The seniors' teacher made sure that the class was on its best behavior. There had been trouble on a recent field trip to the planetarium.

**High-tech facility** Midtown High Senior Class gathered in the science lab to view "the most advanced electron microscope on the Eastern Seaboard."

**Happy snapper** Peter was delighted when M.J. agreed to pose for a few pictures for the school paper. He little knew that a genetically mutated spider was on the loose.

**Struck down**
The bite on Peter's hand looked ugly and swollen by the time he got home. Weak and feverish, he staggered upstairs to his bedroom and collapsed on the floor.

**Super spider** It was M.J. who noticed that one of the lab's 15 genetically mutated spiders was missing. The spiders with their distinctive red and blue coloration combined the jumping abilities of the delena spider, the web-spinning of the funnel-web spider, and the amazing reflexes of the grass spider.

# THE SPIDER
# **FREAK**

Strange things started to happen to Peter Parker in the Midtown High canteen. His fork stuck to his hand, as if caught by microscopic barbs… Then, when he pulled the fork away, a strange, sticky, web-like substance suddenly shot from his wrist and propelled a tray of food all over Flash Thompson, the toughest, meanest guy in the school. In the fight that inevitably followed Peter displayed more superhuman physical powers—dazzling speed, agility, and incredible strength. In just a few minutes, the everyday world of ordinary people and the amazing world of the future Spider-Man had begun to clash.

**Web shot** To Peter's astonishment, the web-like substance attached itself to the lunch tray of a student sitting opposite. Peter ducked as the tray shot past, as if on elastic.

**A mess of trouble**
The tray's contents ended up all over Flash. "Parker?" he growled ominously.

**Fighting mad** Flash tried to punch Peter out, but Peter somehow sensed the blow coming and held Flash in a vice-like grip.

**The loser wins!** M.J. and the other students looked on in awe as the once-puny Peter Parker flung Flash across the room.

**Trial run** With the cry of "Freak!" ringing in his ears, Peter ran into the street, eager to discover more about his new abilities.

**Fateful event** Ben recalled that Peter's odd behavior dated back to the day he came back from a field trip to Columbia University feeling sick.

**Poor excuse** Hearing noises, May knocked anxiously on Peter's bedroom door. Peter told her he was just "exercising."

**Tangled up** Peter's web practice had turned his room into a web-filled mess. Peter wondered what Ben and May would say if they found out.

**Angry words** When Peter announced that he wanted to visit the library, Ben saw a good chance for the pair to have a chat and offered to drive Peter. However, in reality, Peter was heading for a prize-fight in the wrestling ring. Ben tried to discuss the changes Peter was going through. Peter told Ben to stop pretending to be his father.

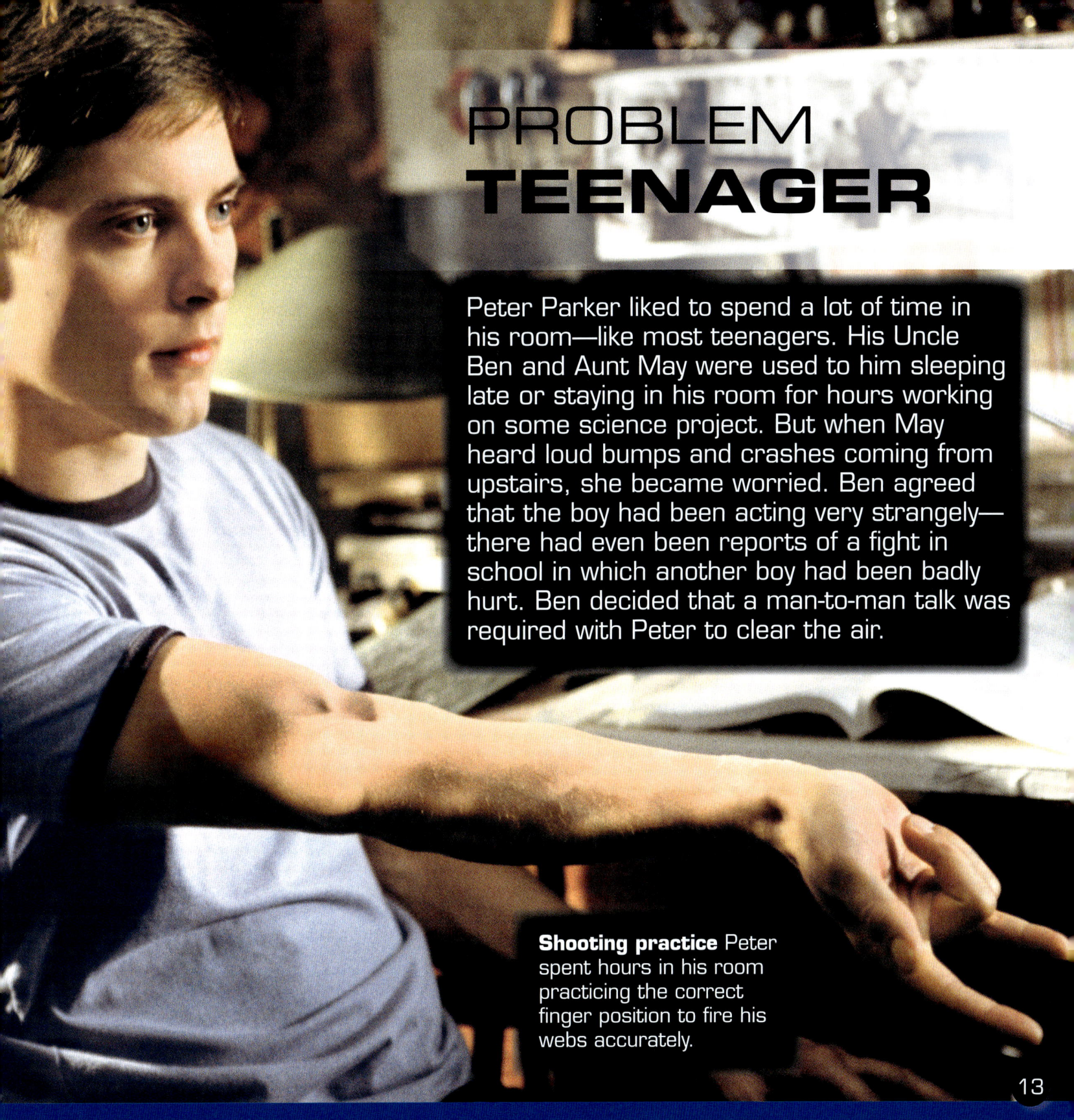

# PROBLEM
# TEENAGER

Peter Parker liked to spend a lot of time in his room—like most teenagers. His Uncle Ben and Aunt May were used to him sleeping late or staying in his room for hours working on some science project. But when May heard loud bumps and crashes coming from upstairs, she became worried. Ben agreed that the boy had been acting very strangely— there had even been reports of a fight in school in which another boy had been badly hurt. Ben decided that a man-to-man talk was required with Peter to clear the air.

**Shooting practice** Peter spent hours in his room practicing the correct finger position to fire his webs accurately.

**Prize-fighter** Peter was sure that he could last three minutes in the wrestling cage with Bone Saw: Master of Disaster and scoop the $3,000 prize.

**Hail the champ!** A few lightning moves later, and Bone Saw was history. The crowd cheered for "The Amazing Spider-Man!" This name was given to Peter Parker by the announcer who didn't think much of Peter's idea of a moniker: "The Human Spider."

**Ripped off** Peter realized that his dreams of buying a car were as far away as ever. Despite promises of big money, all the wrestling promoter gave Peter for his victory was a $100 bill.

# BURDEN OF
# GUILT

With his amazing spider powers, Peter Parker's first thought was to use them to get cash to buy a car to impress M.J. He decided to try and win prize money in the wrestling ring. Uncle Ben seemed to sense that Peter had reached a crossroads in his life and gave him a well-meaning warning: "With great power comes great responsibility." Peter's refusal to heed Ben's words and use his powers to help others would have tragic repercussions.

**Hold up** Peter stood by when a robber snatched the gate money from the promoter.

**The death of Uncle Ben** Peter's inaction allowed the robber to hijack Ben's car, and leave the brave old man to die on the sidewalk.

15

# DREAMS OF
# **STARDOM**

Mary Jane's dreams of a better life seemed to be coming true at last when she landed a part in The Importance of Being Earnest by Oscar Wilde. M.J. hoped that her friends would support her by coming to see the show. Many of them did, including Captain John Jameson, her new boyfriend. Only one person never seemed to have the time, despite his promises—Peter Parker.

**Model career** In addition to the theater role, M.J. featured on a billboard, advertising perfume.

**Full house** The only time M.J. forgot her lines was the night Peter finally kept his promise and took his seat in the stalls.

**Show business** The Lyric was a prestigious off-Broadway theater. A picture of Mary Jane featured prominently on the photograph board outside the theater.

**Who's who?** M.J. and fellow actress Louise played two Victorian ladies who realize that their respective beaus are not who they claim to be.

**Hanging on** The Green Goblin launched an attack on executives from OsCorp as they stood on a balcony. M.J. was also on the balcony as it collapsed. Only a miracle could save her—or Spider-Man.

**First meeting**
M.J wanted to find out who her rescuer was, but Spider-Man did not hang around for long.

**Hopeless love?** His identity finally revealed to Mary Jane, Peter claimed that he would always be Spider-Man: "You and I can never be."

**Moment of truth** M.J.'s brushes with death just made her sure of one thing. It wasn't her rescuer Spider-Man, or rich Harry Osborn, or the astronaut Captain John Jameson she loved—it was Peter Parker.

# M.J. AND SPIDER-MAN

Mary Jane was as brave as she was beautiful—which was just as well as she repeatedly found herself the target of monstrous Super Villains. At first she was attracted to her heroic rescuer Spider-Man. Perhaps she felt that there was something familiar about him. In time, the truth was revealed—Peter Parker was Spider-Man. M.J. was faced with a tough decision: did she want to live a life of comfort with a wealthy husband or one fraught with danger alongside a Super Hero?

**That first kiss**
M.J. kissed Spider-Man, and both their worlds turned upside down.

# A HIGH PRICE
# TO PAY

In time, the Spider Man costume came to symbolize the seemingly thankless, heroic path Peter Parker had chosen. At times, he longed to abandon the costume and all the pain that went with it and just be a normal, anonymous, average guy. However, unforeseen circumstances, the emotional debt he owed Uncle Ben, and his own sense of responsibility always made him reconsider.

**Thrown away** With his life in a mess and his powers failing, Peter chucked his suit in a garbage can.

**Brief relief** Initially Peter was relieved when stress made his powers fail. He got on top of his college work and had time for friends at last. But when Doc Ock attacked M.J., Peter knew only an empowered Spider-Man could save her.

**Inner strength** Unlike the Green Goblin's armored suit, Spider-Man's costume had no special protective powers. Peter relied solely on his own courage and physical skills.

**Behind the mask** Despite all Peter's efforts, the wrong people always found ways of getting to Spider-Man.

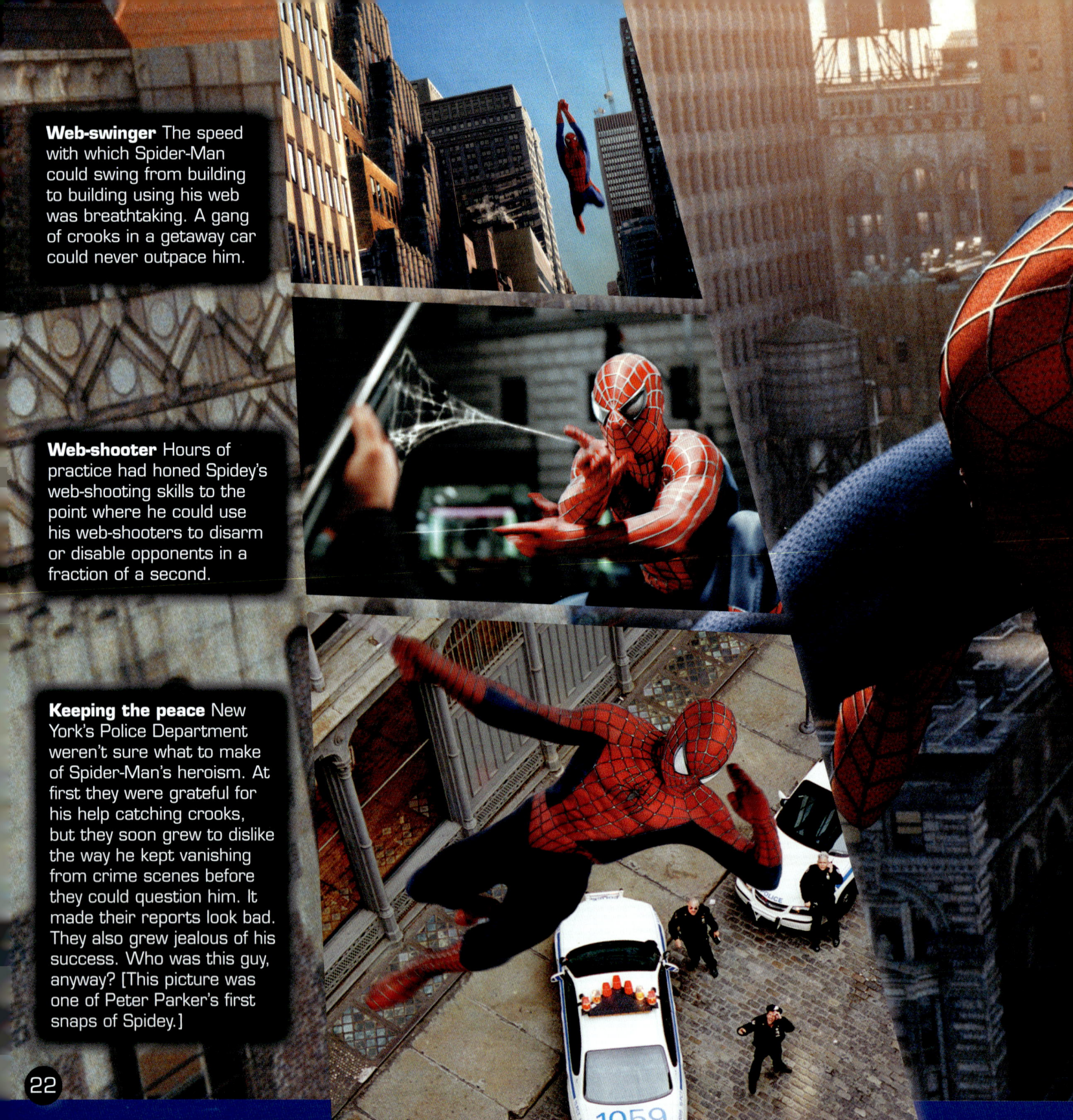

**Web-swinger** The speed with which Spider-Man could swing from building to building using his web was breathtaking. A gang of crooks in a getaway car could never outpace him.

**Web-shooter** Hours of practice had honed Spidey's web-shooting skills to the point where he could use his web-shooters to disarm or disable opponents in a fraction of a second.

**Keeping the peace** New York's Police Department weren't sure what to make of Spider-Man's heroism. At first they were grateful for his help catching crooks, but they soon grew to dislike the way he kept vanishing from crime scenes before they could question him. It made their reports look bad. They also grew jealous of his success. Who was this guy, anyway? [This picture was one of Peter Parker's first snaps of Spidey.]

# SPIDER-MAN'S
# NEW YORK

Swinging and leaping across the skyscraper skyline as Spider-Man, Peter Parker experienced what it was like to feel free for the first time in his life. The whole of New York was suddenly his personal adventure playground, his own turf. Here was where he would make his name as a hero, win public acclaim, defeat Super Villains, and save innocent lives. The city seemed to be a place where, as the amazing Spider-Man, he could fulfill his every dream. And, for a time, it seemed possible that Peter's dreams might come true.

**Battleground** By day or by night, the streets, rooftops, and buildings of New York bore witness to Spidey's unforgettable clashes with Super Villainy.

23

**No comfort** After arriving late at M.J.'s play and seeing her go off with John Jameson, Peter ran off to prowl the rooftops as Spider-Man—only to find that his powers had unaccountably deserted him.

**Hard choice** Two sets of clothes hanging in Peter's closet symbolized his dilemma.

**Goblin games** The Green Goblin tried to confuse Peter by offering to become his ally against the whole world.

**Crash landing** As his psychological pressure built up, Spidey's powers started to cut out, bringing him painfully down to earth.

# SUPER HERO
# SYNDROME

**Poor grades** Peter found combining the roles of Super Hero and science student increasingly difficult.

Peter Parker soon began to realize that being a hero in secret was a heavy burden to carry. The press and the public were eager to discover who Spider-Man was. And so were criminals, desperate for revenge. If they couldn't defeat Spider-Man, they would strike anyone close to him. To protect those he loved, Peter believed he had to keep his identity secret—no matter what the personal cost. The continual stress of leading a double life began to take its toll on Peter...

**Bad blood** Peter's secret role as Spider-Man drove a wedge between himself and Harry Osborn.

**Doctor's advice** Peter tried to explain his situation to Dr. Davis, saying that "his friend" kept dreaming he was Spider-Man and falling. "Maybe you're not supposed to be Spider-Man, climbing those walls," the doctor replied.

**Mixed messages** M.J. was totally confused by Peter's contradictory behavior. Peter couldn't explain himself and, instead, bottled up his feelings.

# SPIDEY SMEARED!

From the outset, J. Jonah Jameson, cynical editor of the *Daily Bugle* had had his doubts about Spider-Man, who was being acclaimed a hero all over town. "Why's he wear a mask? What's he got to hide?" he demanded. "If he doesn't want to be famous, I'll make him infamous!" Jameson soon saw a cunning way of boosting his paper's circulation by orchestrating a campaign against the wall-crawler, falsely accusing him of being in league with Super Villains.

**Smear tactics** The report on the bank job was just one of several stories designed to sully Spider-Man's name.

**Bank heist** When Spider-Man tried to stop Doc Ock from robbing a bank, Jameson spun the story to implicate the web-swinger in the robbery.

**Power loss** The *Daily Bugle* omitted to report that Doc Ock had only got away with his crime because Spider-Man's powers had temporarily failed.

**Name game** Jameson was proud of his striking headlines. He also took credit for many Super Villain names, stating "all these weirdos gotta have a name nowadays!"

**Exhibit A** The *Bugle*'s campaign was partly responsible for Spidey giving up his heroism for a time. When he dumped his costume, it ended up on the *Bugle*'s wall.

**Goblin's visit** Jameson should have been grateful that Spidey was around when the Green Goblin dropped into the *Bugle*'s offices demanding the name of Spider-Man's photographer.

**Wall-climber** Spider-Man's abilities gave him the freedom of the city and allowed him to creep up on the bad guys.

**Fight back** Only the amazing Spider-Man could defeat a powerful urban terrorist like the Green Goblin.

**Crook catcher** Ordinary criminals had little chance against Spidey. He could tackle a city crime wave virtually single-handed.

**Hero or vigilante?** Aunt May believed that heroes "set examples for all of us" but J. Jonah Jameson thought that heroes like Spider-Man were "a public menace."

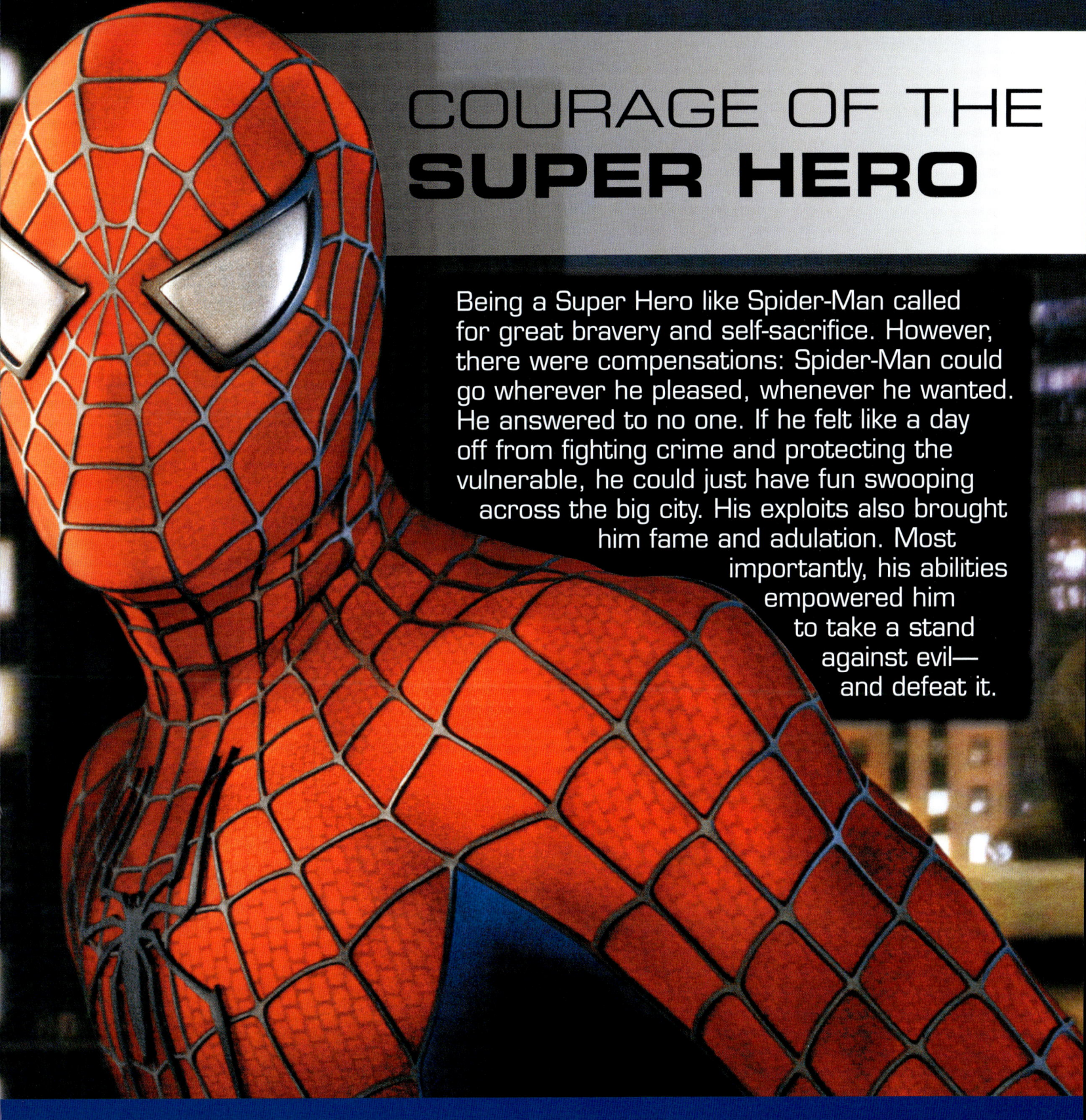

# COURAGE OF THE
# SUPER HERO

Being a Super Hero like Spider-Man called for great bravery and self-sacrifice. However, there were compensations: Spider-Man could go wherever he pleased, whenever he wanted. He answered to no one. If he felt like a day off from fighting crime and protecting the vulnerable, he could just have fun swooping across the big city. His exploits also brought him fame and adulation. Most importantly, his abilities empowered him to take a stand against evil— and defeat it.

# THE GREEN GOBLIN

When Norman Osborn took a dose of his serum it turned him into a super-strong killer. The effects soon wore off and he repressed the memory of his murderous actions for a while. However, he could not resist the sense of overwhelming power that the drug gave him. He became the Green Goblin, equipped with an armored suit, mask, and an array of weaponry. Mounted on his Goblin Glider, he attacked anyone who blocked his path to glory, including the US Army, the board of OsCorp, and Spider-Man.

**Team-up** The Goblin knew that Spider-Man was the only one who could stop him. He decided to make an ally of him. Together they would be unstoppable.

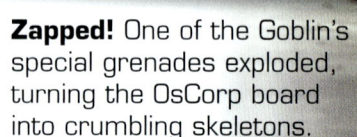

**Zapped!** One of the Goblin's special grenades exploded, turning the OsCorp board into crumbling skeletons.

**Betrayal** Osborn was furious when the OsCorp board voted him out. They had accepted a tender offer from rival company Quest.

**Explosive debut** The Goblin attacked Quest's test for a new exoskeleton for troops to use. The villain detroyed the prototype and US Army personnel, including General Slocum.

**Powerless**
Police vainly tried to stop the Goblin turning OsCorp's World Unity Day into a scene of carnage and chaos.

**Green power** The Goblin's equipment was designed by Osborn himself. He wore a fully articulated armored battlesuit. Special devices in the gauntlets released sleep-inducing or poisonous gas. He also used a variety of bombs and explosive devices. One of his devices shot out bolts with whirling, razor-sharp blades. The jet-powered glider was equipped with rockets, machine guns, and retractable blades.

# ACCIDENTAL DEATH

The Green Goblin was furious that Spider-Man had refused to join with him against the world. "Misery, misery, that's what you've chosen," the Goblin sneered. "I offered you friendship and you spat in my face!" After the Goblin had terrorized a tramload of passengers and Mary Jane, the stage was set for a final showdown between Super Hero and Super Villain, from which only one would emerge the winner.

**Showdown** The Goblin weakened Spider-Man by attacking those he loved: Aunt May and M.J. He went in for the kill wielding his special trident. But Spider-Man was not finished yet…

**Goblin grenade** Osborn had a vast supply of weaponry, which he kept in a secret room in his mansion.

**Battle joined** The Goblin first faced Spidey at OsCorp's World Unity Fair. Spider-Man had got the better of the duel, winning the Goblin's respect.

**Knockout gas** The Goblin cunningly avoided taking on Spider-Man in combat at the *Bugle* offices. Instead, he subdued him with a paralyzing gas from his gloves.

**The Goblin scorned** The Goblin was enraged by Spider-Man's rejection. "No one says no to me!" he shouted. He immediately began plotting his revenge.

**Last gasp** Defeated, Osborn took off his mask to confuse Peter and deny all responsibility for the Goblin's crimes. The trick nearly worked, but Osborn impaled himself on his glider's blades.

# HOSPITAL
# MURDER

Dr. Otto Octavius's fusion experiment to provide electricity had been a disaster. If Spider-Man had not turned off the power, an explosion would have resulted that could have destroyed the city. Octavius's wife, Rosie, was dead and he himself had received an electric shock that had fused his four artificially intelligent mechanical tentacles to his body. As doctors prepared to operate, no one realized that the inhibitor chip that enabled Octavius's brain to control the arms was no longer in place.

**System unstable** The audience looked on with mounting terror as the fusion reaction went into overload. The scientist had made a serious error in his calculations.

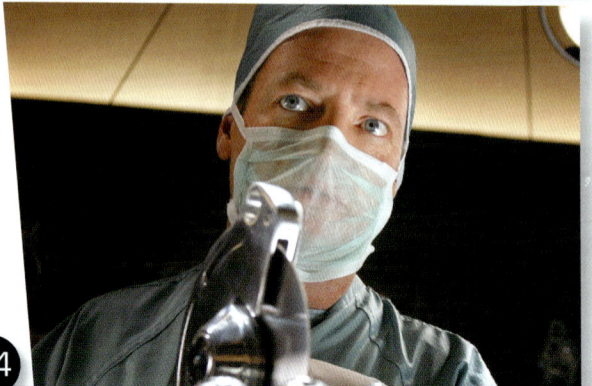

**Saw point** A surgeon prepared to cut the metal arms from Octavius's body.

**Dire emergency** The arms refused to be separated from their host and viciously attacked the medical team.

**Awful truth** Octavius awoke and was horrified at the carnage his arms had wrought.

**On the loose** Controlled by his smart arms, the helpless Octavius was propelled into the streets of Manhattan.

# DOC OCK:
# DOWNFALL

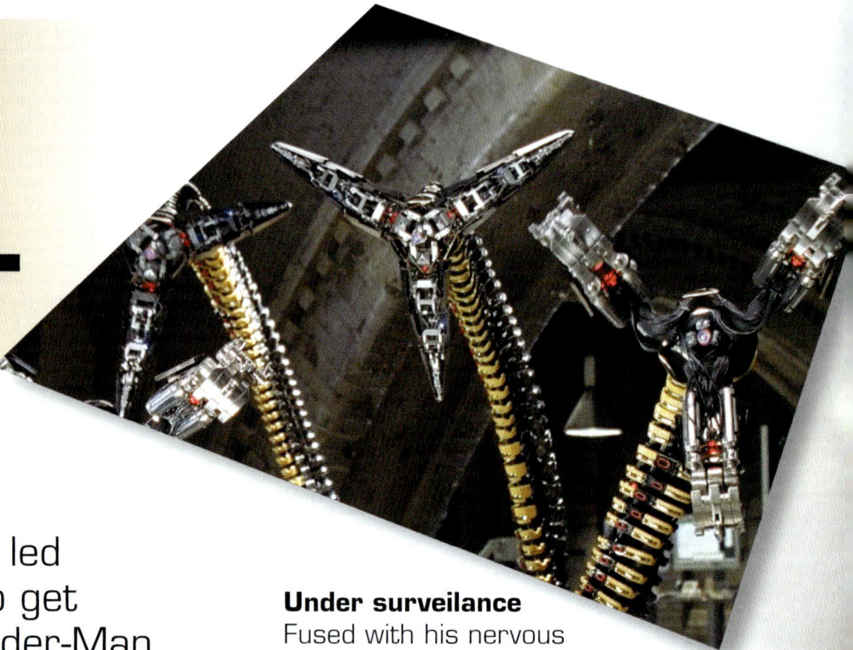

The half-crazed Dr. Octavius was driven on by his arms' promptings to continue his perilous fusion research. His need for more tritium from OsCorp led him to Harry Osborn. Osborn agreed to get him the mineral if he would capture Spider-Man, whom Harry hated for his part in the death of his father, Norman. Doc Ock's trail of destruction would endanger Peter Parker, put M.J.'s life in the balance, and threaten half of New York. It would also lead to Octavius's own suicide.

**Under surveilance**
Fused with his nervous system, Octavius's snakelike arms overrode his human side, persuading him that any means were justifiable to continue his work.

**Riverside base**
Doc Ock rebuilt his lab in an abandoned warehouse sited on a pier jutting into the Hudson River.

**Final reckoning** Doc Ock had kidnapped M.J. and was prepared to kill her to stop her informing on him. However, Spider-Man infiltrated Doc Ock's base, defeated him, and saved M.J. before the villain destroyed half the city with his fusion reactor.

**Crisis of conscience** A last minute appeal by Peter Parker persuaded Octavius to shut down his experiment. The only way to do this was to hurl the fusion machine into the river. With the words, "I will not die a monster," Octavius followed his life's work into watery oblivion.

37

# VENGEANCE AND
# BETRAYAL

Former friends can make the bitterest enemies. Harry Osborn had envied Peter Parker all his life. But this jealousy was nothing compared to his hatred for Spider-Man, Peter's friend. After the death of his father, Norman Osborn, in battle with Spider-Man as the Green Goblin, Harry became consumed with dreams of revenge. Haunted by his father's ghost, Harry made a pact with the villain Doc Octopus, offering research help in exchange for capturing Spider-Man. The plot failed, but Harry discovered Spider-Man's true identity. Henceforth Peter Parker would be his target.

**Party pooper**
A drunken Harry accused Peter of shielding Spider-Man from the law.

**Murder for science**
Doc Octopus agreed to capture Spider-Man in exchange for tritium to continue his experiments.

**The revelation** Doctor Octopus dumped Spider-Man at Harry's mansion. Harry seized a dagger and ripped off Spidey's mask...

**Gothic gloom**
Harry had moved back into his father Norman's mansion, a 19th-century building with a sinister, brooding atmosphere.

**Voice of evil** The ghost of Norman Osborn led Harry to the secret room containing the Green Goblin's weaponry, whispering, "Be strong, Harry. Avenge Me!"

'THE GREATEST
BATTLE LIES
WITHIN.'

# BATTLING WITH
# THE DARKNESS

**Personality crisis** The black suit seemed to urge Peter to throw off his sense of right and wrong, and to revel in power for its own sake.

Peter Parker and Harry Osborn had more in common than their friendship and a mutual love of M.J. Both faced daunting battles with personal demons. Peter was assailed by an alien threat. It turned his red and blue Spider-Man costume black and brought him increased powers, but it also threatened to turn him into a monster. Harry was still prey to visitations from his father's phantom, urging Harry to follow in the Green Goblin footsteps, avenge his death, and kill Spidey. Somehow Peter and Harry had to defeat their dark sides to regain their souls.

**Face of evil** Harry was unable to resist the call of the Goblin's mask, promising him power and revenge over Spider-Man.

**The New Goblin** A new masked enemy was out to finish Spider-Man, mounted on a high-tech glider shaped like a snowboard.

**A restless night** Peter was exhausted by recent battles with new Super Villains and rows with M.J.

**Out of the shadows** An alien black substance crept over Spider-Man as he slept and merged with his costume.

**Into the black** The new suit gave Spider-Man even greater fighting powers, but it also threatened to take over his mind and dominate his every move. Peter Parker was engaged in an inner struggle far tougher than any fight with a criminal could be.

**Split personality** As the black costume took hold of Spider-Man's mind, he began to lose his sense of identity. What kind of a hero was he?

**Power-packed** The red and blue Spider-Man would have struggled to combat the latest villain. Spidey convinced himself that he *needed* the black suit's powers.

# STORM OF
# THE SANDMAN

Pursued by the law, Flint Marko stumbled into the middle of a scientific test that would turn an ordinary criminal into a Super Villain. Every molecule in his body was converted into sand particles, which he could adapt into any shape or hardness he pleased. Marko became the Sandman, a terrifying creature of immense power, who could disassemble his sand body to pass through, over, or under any barrier. The Sandman embarked on a one-man sandstorm of crime. Only Spider-Man could take on Sandman and reduce him to a puddle of mud.

**Shifting sands** The scientific test had bombarded Marko with radiation, giving him extraordinary powers. A punch from Spider-Man passed harmlessly through his sand body and out the other side. He was virtually invulnerable.

**Second chances** The black-suited Spider-Man later spotted Marko escaping with the loot from a bank robbery. Spider-Man chased Marko into the subway. This time, the enhanced powers of the black suit gave him more chance of defeating the Sandman.

**Dunes of doom** Sandman could enter a building, such as a bank or hospital, as Flint Marko. But if there was any trouble inside he could leave as Sandman, engulfing and crushing anything and anyone in his way. Police were swallowed in a blinding sandstorm.

**Chimes of freedom** Peter Parker realized that the black suit was turning him into a heartless monster. His behaviour had alienated M.J. and if he ever wanted to win her back he had to be rid of it. Alone in a church steeple, he tore frantically at the suit, but it seemed stuck to his skin. Then the church bells began to ring out...

**Inside the church**, Eddie Brock uttered a fervent prayer: "It's Brock sir, Edward Brock, Jr. I'm here humbled and humiliated to ask you for one thing... I want you to kill Peter Parker." His prayer was soon answered, though not in the way he could have expected.

# THE VICIOUSNESS
## OF VENOM

Photographer Eddie Brock's professional reputation was in tatters: he had been exposed as a fraud. Pictures that claimed to show a black-costumed Spider-Man robbing a bank had been exposed as fakes by Peter Parker. Utterly humiliated, Brock swore to be avenged. A bizarre encounter with Peter gave Brock the chance to achieve his aim, to focus all his pent-up poison, hatred, and rage as if he had become possessed by a dark, alien force of evil. A new power swept over him: the power of Venom.

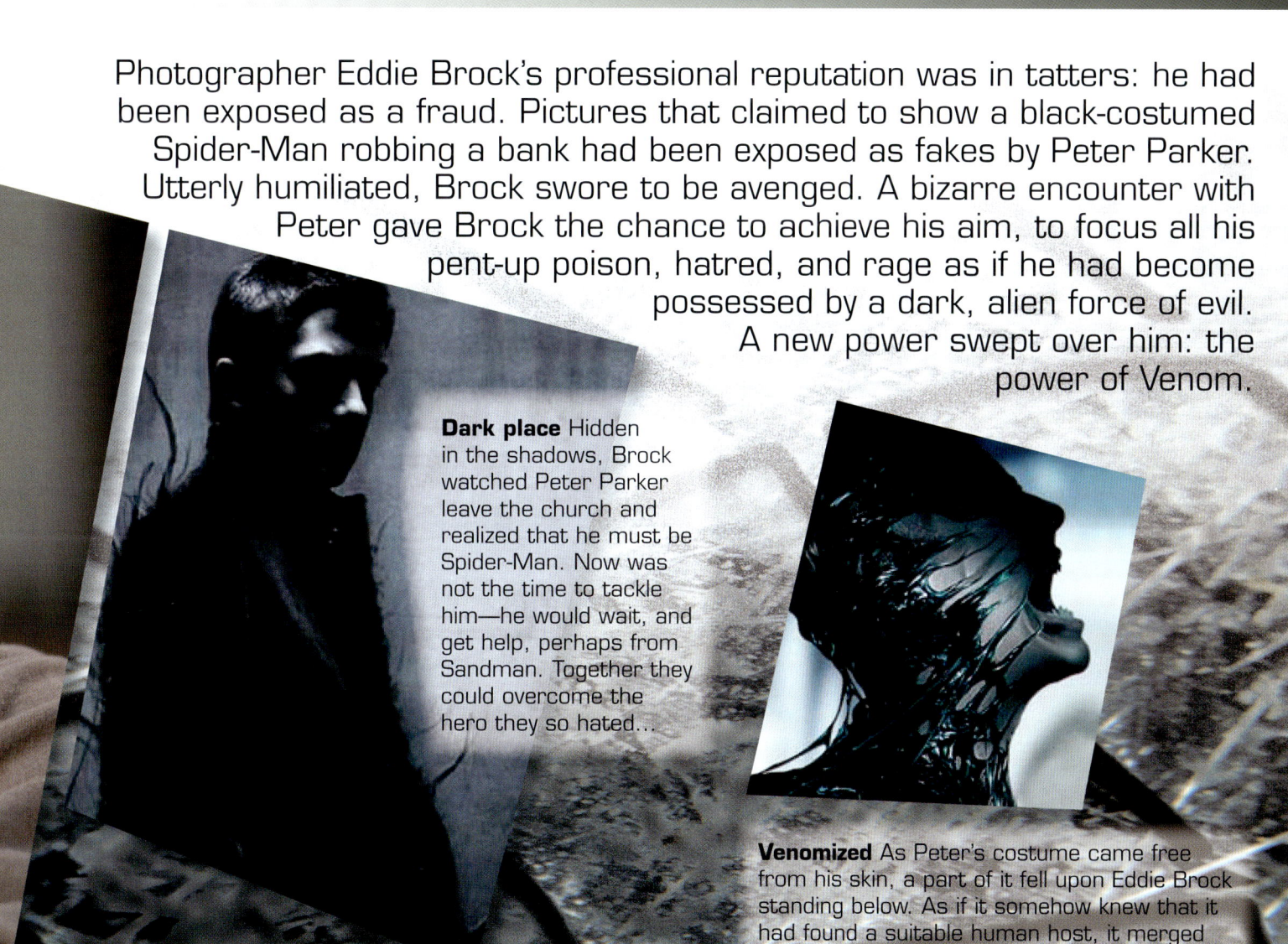

**Dark place** Hidden in the shadows, Brock watched Peter Parker leave the church and realized that he must be Spider-Man. Now was not the time to tackle him—he would wait, and get help, perhaps from Sandman. Together they could overcome the hero they so hated...

**Venomized** As Peter's costume came free from his skin, a part of it fell upon Eddie Brock standing below. As if it somehow knew that it had found a suitable human host, it merged with him in seconds. Under the influence of the strange alien material, Eddie Brock would become the bloodthirsty Super Villain Venom.

# SPIDER-MAN™

## THE VISUAL GUIDE TO THE COMPLETE MOVIE TRILOGY
## EVERYBODY LOVES A HERO

# SPIDER-MAN

## THE VISUAL GUIDE TO THE

### COMPLETE MOVIE TRILOGY

Written by Alastair Dougall

# BOOK ONE:
# EVERYBODY LOVES A HERO

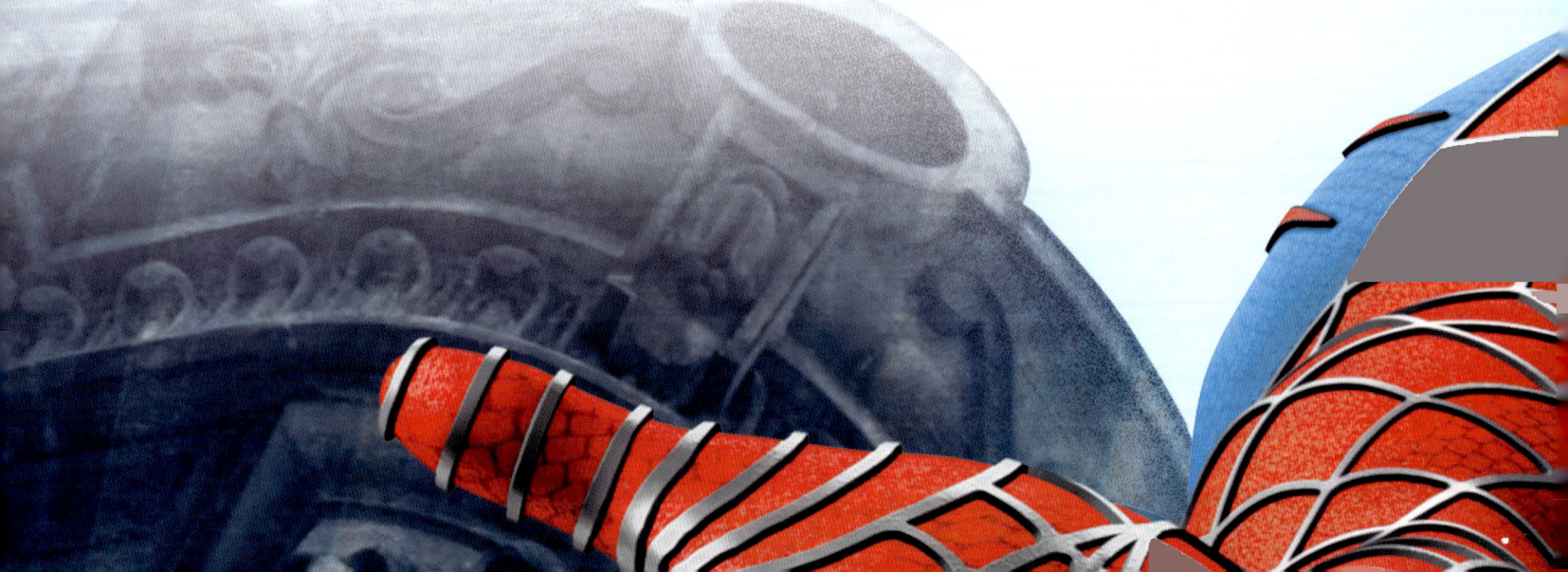

"Who am I? You sure you want to know? The story of my life is not for the faint of heart. If somebody said it was a happy little tale, if somebody told you I was just your average, ordinary guy, not a care in the world… somebody lied…"

# PETER
# PARKER

It would be hard to find anyone less cut out to become a Super Hero than Peter Parker. He was the boy no one wanted to sit next to on the school bus, an outsider, an orphan who lived with his aunt and uncle. He wore big glasses, had a puny build, and came across as awkward and nervous. The fact that he was also a "whiz" at science just made him more of a target for the tough kids in his high-school class. One of the few who appreciated Peter's sensitivity and intelligence was "M.J.," Mary Jane Watson, but Peter was so shy he hardly dared speak to her. Why would such a pretty, popular girl want to go out with him?

**Face of an angel**
Peter had been crazy about M.J., the girl next door, ever since he was six years old. The first time he saw her he asked his Aunt May, "Is that an angel?"

## Late as usual

Peter's head was so filled with his latest science project and thoughts of M.J. that he always ended up running desperately for the school bus. "Stop the bus!" shouted M.J. "He's been chasing us since Woodhaven Boulevard!"

## Figure of fun

Peter was only too aware that the other students thought he was a joke. Even the bus driver was laughing as he brought the bus to a halt, allowing Peter to stumble breathlessly aboard.

## High-school graduation

Peter's academic talents were finally recognized when he won the science award. He posed happily for pictures for the high-school paper. As soon as the pictures were taken, the students flung their mortar boards high in the air.

## Flash Thompson

The star athlete of Midtown High, Flash Thomspn didn't think much of a geek like Peter Parker. He thought M.J. was his girl and lucky to be so.

## Harry Osborn

Harry was Peter's best friend. Unfortunately, Harry was also attracted to M.J. If Peter was too tongue-tied to talk to her, Harry certainly wasn't. And if he could impress her with a few scraps of knowledge picked up from Peter, so much the better!

# DAWNING OF
# A NEW DAY

Peter awoke. The feverish sickness that had overwhelmed him the night before had completely vanished—he'd made a lightning recovery. Even more amazing, for the first time that he could recall, he didn't need glasses. He glanced in the mirror: overnight he had somehow acquired the muscles of an Olympic gymnast! Surfing a sudden wave of self-confidence, he promised himself that today was the day he would pluck up the courage to ask M.J. on a date...

**20/20 vision** Perfect eyesight was just the first of many physical changes Peter would experience that day.

**Reflex action** In the Midtown canteen, Peter dazzled M.J. with his rapid responses, saving her from falling and also catching her tray. She was clearly impressed, but still went to sit next to her boyfriend Flash Thompson.

**Freelance snapper** Peter "spider-walked" downstairs, astonishing Ben and May with his energy. Only last night he'd looked dead on his feet! Peter left for school promising to help Uncle Ben paint the kitchen that evening. "Don't start without me!" he shouted. "Teenagers," Ben sighed.

# AT HOME WITH
# BEN AND MAY

**Peaceful neighborhood** Ben, May, and Peter Parker lived in the quiet New York suburb of Queens.

Peter Parker was well aware that he owed a great deal to his Uncle Ben and Aunt May. His parents had died when he was young and Ben and May had not only looked after the orphan, they had treated him like the son they had wished for but never had. Ben and May never had much money and, at times, had to struggle to make ends meet. But however tough things got, their mutual love and respect saw them through.

**Out of work** Ben had lost his job as an electrician and was worred whether, aged 68, he would be able to get another.

**Father figure** Ben was well aware that Peter needed guidance to help him through the "difficult" teenage years. Ben was determined to instill in Peter the same strong moral values that he had always lived by.

**Loyal wife** May had great confidence in her husband. "We've been down and out before, but somehow we survive," she smiled.

**On the bright side**
May's outlook was optimistic and cheerful. She was wonderfully supportive of her husband and Peter, and immensely proud of them both.

**The handyman**
Ben's only outlet for his electrical skills was repairing household appliances.

# POWERS OF
# THE SPIDER

Peter Parker realized that something life-changing had happened to him. Were his sudden amazing powers his for good, or just a one-off event? Could he make them come back at will? These questions raced through his mind as he ran from the Midtown schoolyard into the quiet of a deserted alley. He needed time to think. He needed time to learn how to control his spider powers, or his life would be ruined and they would end up controlling him!

**Telltale signs** Peter concentrated hard—and microscopic hairs protruded from his pores.

**Effort of will** Peter suspected it could take many hours to master his new super abilities.

**Spider grip** Seen up close, the hairs were equipped with tiny barbs that could grip onto any surface.

**Spider web** A weird, spider-shaped mark on his wrist was the only sign of Peter's web-shooting power.

**The wallcrawler** The barbs on his hands combined with his superhuman spider strength enabled Peter to climb a wall in seconds. Utterly exhilarated, he glanced back at the ground below.

**High-tensile action**
Peter's web was so strong, it supported his weight with ease, allowing him to swing like a latterday Tarzan from building to building.

# A GIRL CALLED M.J.

Mary Jane Watson seemed to have everything going for her. She was intelligent, pretty, and popular. However, the truth was not so rosy. Her father's frequent abusive rages undermined her sense of self-worth. She longed to escape the dreary life that fate seemed to have mapped out for her. Maybe a glamorous boyfriend could be the answer...

**Thinking it over**

M.J. usually concealed her feelings as she wasn't sure who to trust. She had a secret plan: she would become an actress—and a star.

**Big bully** Flash Thompson was M.J.'s high-school boyfriend, but she tired of his arrogant, intimidating ways. Flash drove a fancy car, but had little else to recommend him!

**Few prospects** M.J.'s dreams of a better life always seemed to stay just that—dreams! She worked as a waitress at the Moondance Diner but the job was grinding her down. She'd had her fill of being nagged by the boss and hassled by customers.

**The right stuff?** M.J. wondered if she had found her Mr. Right when astronaut Captain John Jameson fell for her. He was handsome and heroic, but was he just too perfect?

# MARY JANE
# AND PETER

Peter Parker had been in love with Mary Jane Watson since she moved in next door when he was six years old. However, he never had the nerve to tell her. Mary Jane had been in love with Peter Parker for years but never realized it. Throw a secret Super Hero identity into the mix for the perfect recipe for a turbulent romance!

**Someone else** M.J. told Peter that she was now dating his friend Harry Osborn.

**Lost cause** As far as M.J. was concerned, Peter always turned up too late. At least John Jameson was punctual.

**Dead flowers** Peter bought M.J. carnations for her play. But he arrived late and never gave them to her.

**Wrong time** Peter had resolved to give up being Spider-Man and asked M.J. to "pick up where we left off." He was too late again—M.J. had agreed to marry Captain John Jameson.

**Love lost** M.J told Peter she loved him, but he said he could be no more than a friend.

**Lonely hero** Peter knew that being Spider-Man placed anyone close to him in danger, so he rejected M.J.

**Runaway bride** M.J. left Jameson at the altar to be with Peter. M.J. and Peter were together at last, but for how long?

**Telltale sign** M.J. realized it was Peter, not Jameson, whom she loved. She asked Peter for a kiss so she would know if he really loved her.

19

**Rough sketch** In Peter's first designs, the costume had a cape and utility belt—like another famous hero.

# THE COSTUME
# OF A HERO

**Looking good** The wrestling ad specified that colorful characters were a must.

Peter Parker originally designed his costume for his debut in the wrestling ring as "The Human Spider." Its red and blue colors recalled the spider that bit and empowered Peter. His first homemade effort was ill-fitting—no wonder the wrestling crowd laughed! However, he soon devised a snug bodysuit of stretch fabric with a hood that completely masked his face—a costume fit for a Super Hero.

**Design into reality** Peter found that turning his design into a costume was not a simple task. He initially adapted old clothes. The results weren't great, but the outfit would just have to do.

**Powerful symbol** After several attempts, Peter came up with a cool, stylized spider logo.

**Into the night** Thoughts of impressing M.J. spurred Peter on as he worked. Bit by bit, an effective design began to take shape.

**Costumed hero** Peter's fully realized design fitted like a second skin, although he admitted that it did have a tendency to feel "kinda itchy."

**In action** Peter may have looked weird, with a wrinkled mask that showed his eyes, but victory won him the wrestling crowd's respect.

**Hero in a mask** The mask was the most important part of the costume, completely hiding Peter's face. This allowed him total freedom as long as no one found out his true identity.

# PETER PARKER'S
# NEW YORK

**The A grade student**
When Peter applied himself, he shone on his college science course. However, his tutor, Dr. Connors, couldn't understand why his work was so erratic.

At first, the Big Apple seemed an intimidating place to Peter Parker; nevertheless, he was determined to prove himself in this unforgiving city of hard-nosed deals and sudden dangers. Peter felt more at home when Manhattan's hustle and bustle gave way to the sleepy suburb of Queens. It was there he grew up, in a safe, friendly, close-knit neighborhood, cared for by his Uncle Ben and Aunt May. It was there he went to high school. And it was there he fell for the pretty girl next door, Mary Jane Watson.

**Freelance snapper** Peter had ambitions to make it as a photographer and had gained useful experience taking pictures for his high-school paper.

**Always broke** Peter moved to a one-room apartment, but struggled to pay the rent.

**Pizza delivery** Without rich parents to support him, Peter had to work his way through college. Unfortunately, Spider-Man heroics and a regular job didn't mix well.

**Safe and secure** The home that Peter grew up in was a place of old-fashioned moral values.

**Photo opportunity** *Daily Bugle* editor J. Jonah Jameson gave Peter work as a photographer, but only if he could get pictures of Spider-Man.

**At the ready** Beneath his normal clothes, Peter Parker wore the red and blue of Spider-Man.

# NEIGHBORHOOD
# HERO

Modestly describing himself as "your friendly neighborhood Spider-Man," the amazing wall-crawler performed headlining deeds, chasing down violent criminals and bringing them to justice. He was also on hand to save children from certain death. Before long, the whole of New York was hailing his bravery. Even buskers sang his praises. For a while, everyone was grateful for the mysterious hero who had appeared in their midst.

**Grateful parent** Spider-Man miraculously rescued a baby that had seemed sure to die in a fire.

**Children first** Even when attacked by the Green Goblin, Spider-Man never forgot his heroic priorities, risking his life to save a child from being crushed by a giant inflatable.

**Spider-powers**
Spidey's strength, speed, agility, and "spider-sense" enabled him to go where no fireman or policeman ever could—and get out alive.

**Truly amazing** Police looked on in wonder as Spider-Man brought in yet another felon who had escaped their grasp.

**Friendly warning** Spidey advised children against everyday dangers, such as crossing roads.

# J. JONAH JAMESON

**The office** When Jameson was out, the atmosphere at the *Bugle* was calm, reflecting the office's old-fashioned decor.

Everyone who worked at the *Daily Bugle*, New York's biggest tabloid, knew who the boss was: J. Jonah Jameson. He had worked his way up from copy boy to editor, but success hadn't mellowed him. This irritable, workaholic skinflint relished making staff squirm with a sarcastic comment or panicking them with an outburst. When rookie Peter Parker said that he could get pictures of Spider-Man, Jameson saw the chance of a sensational scoop at a knock-down price.

**Eyes on the prize** Jameson wanted to exploit the Spidey story for all it was worth.

**Cut rate** Peter was bullied into accepting only $300 for his exclusive Spider-Man photographs.

**Money talks** Jameson had three obsessions: scooping his rivals, selling papers, and watching every last cent.

**Money-maker** Peter had been attracted to the *Daily Bugle* by an ad Jameson had placed.

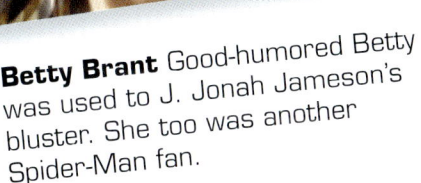

**Robbie Robertson** The *Bugle*'s City Editor, Robertson was a supporter of Spider-Man—unlike his boss.

**Hoffman** With his perpetually anxious expression, Hoffman was a staffer whom Jameson enjoyed shouting at.

**Betty Brant** Good-humored Betty was used to J. Jonah Jameson's bluster. She too was another Spider-Man fan.

**Friendly face** Betty Brant, Jameson's secretary, took a shine to Peter and helped him out with an advance whenever she could.

**An unstoppable force** Robbie and Hoffman knew that questioning Jameson's decisions, however eccentric, was usually hopeless. Press ethics meant nothing to the boss.

# AUNT MAY:
# TRUE HEROISM

**Consolation** May forgot her own pain to comfort Peter after Ben's funeral.

Fearful of losing Aunt May's love, Peter was unable to confess his guilt over Uncle Ben's death. He buried his shame by performing heroic deeds as Spider-Man. He knew that one day he would have to tell May how he had stood by and let a violent criminal escape and kill Ben. Ben's death left May heartbroken and in dire financial straits. However, she remained the one person Peter could rely on for unfailing support.

**Love and support** Aunt May had been like a mother to Peter, encouraging him through his high-school years. She was delighted when he won the Science Award.

**Attack of the Goblin** May was terrified when the Green Goblin smashed his way into her house searching for Peter.

**Good advice** While recovering in hospital, May assured Peter that M.J. loved him.

**Money troubles** May was unable to get a bank loan to meet her mortgage payments.

**United in grief** May and Peter bore Ben's death with great bravery. As the inscription on the gravestone read, Ben was a beloved husband and uncle.

**Fighting back** May played her part in defeating Doc Ock when the villain took her hostage.

**Confession** Peter eventually found the courage to tell May about the events leading up to Ben's death and she forgave him.

**Moving on** May resolved to solve her financial plight by giving up the family home and moving to a small apartment.

**A true heroine** Selfless, loyal, brave, and wise, May had all the attributes of heroism, without the costumed hero's glamorous trappings.

29

# NORMAN
# OSBORN

The head of OsCorp Industries, Norman Osborn, was a scientific genius whose research was funded by the US military. He had produced a powered, one-man glider, but his pet project was a drug designed to enhance human performance and turn ordinary fighting men into super-soldiers. However, recent experiments had revealed disturbing side effects and the army chief wanted to pull Osborn's funding. Determined to prove his serum a success, Osborn resolved to try it on himself.

**Progress report** General Slocum was unimpressed to hear of problems with the human enhancement program.

**Test subject** Given just two weeks to prove the that serum worked, Osborn decided desperate measures were called for.

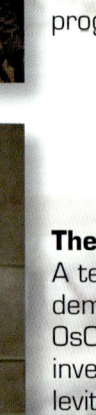

**The Glider** A technician demonstrated OsCorp's latest invention: a levitating glider.

**Chamber of horrors** Osborn's assistant, Dr. Stromm, strapped Osborn onto the lab gurney and performance enhancer chemicals filled the chamber.

**Flawed genius** Osborn was a brilliant man, but he was arrogant, paranoid, and had scant regard for others. He persuaded himself that the failure of his performance enhancer project would mean the downfall of OsCorp. It was this instability that contributed to OsCorp's directors voting him off the board—a blow to his ego that he was determined to avenge.

**Side effect** Dr. Stromm tried to resuscitate Osborn. Moments later, Stromm was fighting for his life as Osborn became a raging madman.

# A DEADLY
## SECRET

Norman Osborn had always had a lot of respect for Peter Parker, both for his scientific promise and for his determination to make his own way in the world. Norman liked self-reliant achievers, like himself. His murderous alter ego the Green Goblin valued the same qualities, which was why he wanted to make a pact with Spider-Man. Norman never suspected that Peter and the wall-crawler could be one and the same, until certain events aroused his suspicions…

**Father's favorite** Norman regarded Peter almost as a second son. His real son, Harry, had been given every advantage but had been a disappointment.

**Job offer** During the time Peter shared an apartment with Harry, Norman offered Peter a job. Peter declined and Norman was impressed that Peter chose to stand on his own feet.

**Missing person** Aunt May, Harry, and Norman wondered why Peter was late for Thanksgiving dinner. Peter was hiding above their heads in his Spider-Man costume. He had just returned from a battle with the Green Goblin, during which he had been cut on the arm by the Goblin's pumpkin blade.

**Blood simple** As Norman was about to carve the turkey, he noticed a telltale scratch on Peter's arm. He immediately realized that Peter was Spider-Man.

# DOCTOR OCTAVIUS

Doctor Otto Octavius was determined to place his scientific genius at the service of humanity. His latest project, financed by OsCorp, was his most ambitious: a new kind of fusion reactor, a "perpetual sun" providing vast amounts of electricity safely and cheaply. He staged a demonstration before an invited audience, which included Harry Osborn and Peter Parker. Dr. Octavius used his four mechanical arms attached to his body to manipulate the reaction. But the reaction proved unstable, creating a power surge. His wife, Rosie, was killed and Otto was hospitalized.

**Rosie Octavius** Otto's wife, Rosie, was his rock. He had wooed her with poetry, and suggested Peter do the same to win his "secret love."

**Octavius's credo** Peter was writing a paper on Octavius's work and he visited the doctor's lab. Octavius warned Peter against laziness, saying, "Intelligence is not a privilege, it's a gift."

**Ring of confidence** Octavius thanked OsCorp Industries for providing the precious mineral tritium to fuel his reactor. Harry Osborn, now in charge of Special Projects at OsCorp, was convinced that Otto would win a Nobel Prize.

**Under control** Otto explained that an inhibitor chip helped him to control his mechanical arms' artificial intelligence.

**Unstable reaction** As equipment short-circuited, Otto tried to reassure the audience.

# REIGN OF
# TERROR

**Smash and grab**
Doc Ock's smart arms tore a bank vault door off its hinges and flung it across the lobby. It just missed Aunt May and Peter Parker.

A new terrifying Super Villain was at large in New York City. Dubbed "Doc Ock" by the *Daily Bugle*, he had four mechanical arms of incredible destructive power that seemed to grow out of his back. The story was that Doc Ock had once been a philanthropic scientist until an experiment had failed and he had gone crazy, killing doctors who were trying to save his life. Police were powerless to prevent his rampages, which included robbing a bank. Even Spider-Man had been unable to stop him...

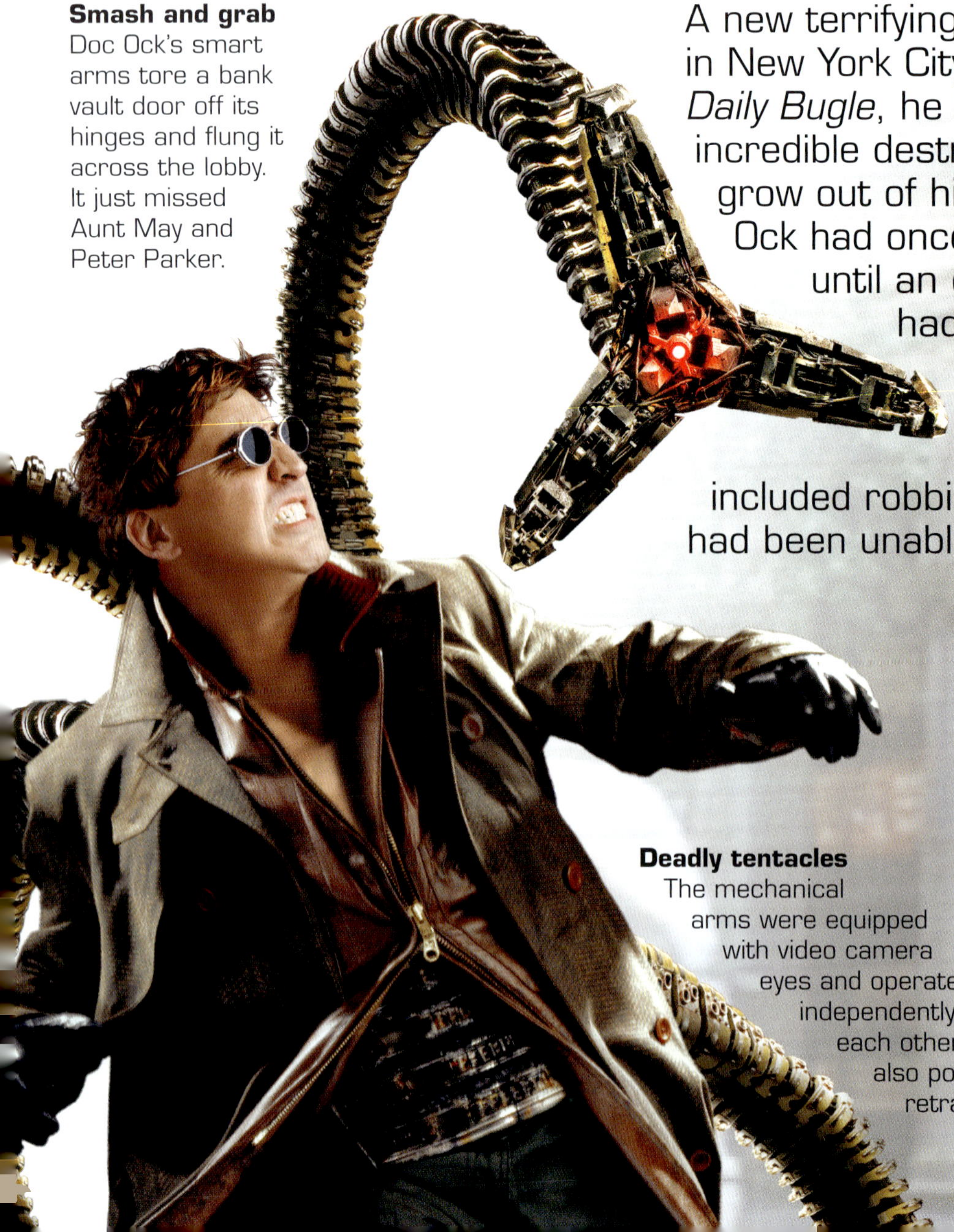

**Deadly tentacles**
The mechanical arms were equipped with video camera eyes and operated independently of each other. They also possessed retractable spikes.

**Doc Ock's agenda**
No one realized it at the time, but Doc Ock robbed the bank to get money to continue his fusion research.

**Smart weapons** Doc Ock's arms were designed to perform delicate scientific operations. But their pincers had awesome crushing power.

**Fighting back**
Speed was Spidey's best defense against Doc Ock's tentacles. Made of a virtually indestructible alloy, the arms were as flexible as snakes.

**Caught up** A sudden loss of Spider-Man's powers enabled Doc Ock to gain the upper hand. However, Spidey soon broke free.

# HARRY
# OSBORN

**Pleasing Dad** Harry's failure to impress the father he worshipped made him insecure. Harry often had to rely on Peter's help to keep up his college grades.

Harry Osborn was once Peter Parker's best friend. Like Peter, Harry had no mother, and his wealthy background had made him an outsider. His father, the famous scientist Norman Osborn, was domineering and difficult to please. The fact that his dad seemed to think more of Peter than him made Harry jealous. Another source of rivalry was Mary Jane Watson. At first Harry impressed M.J. with his wealthy background, but in his heart he knew that it was Peter she loved.

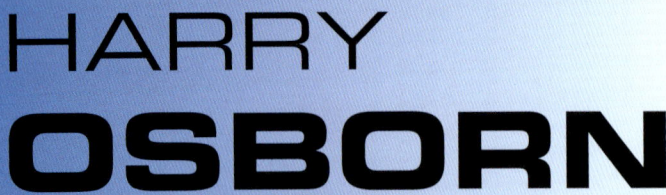

**Source of tension** Harry was only too aware that his father was impressed by Peter's character and academic achievements.

38

**Romancing M.J.** On the field trip to Columbia University's spider lab, Harry impressed M.J., the prettiest girl in the school, with knowledge he had gleaned from Peter Parker.

**Pulling away** Harry was disappointed when M.J. didn't wear black—a color his father loved—at the OsCorp World Unity Fair. She wanted to be her own person, and hated being kissed in public! The relationship broke up when Norman Osborn accused M.J. of being a golddigger after Harry's trust fund.

**Vow of revenge** Harry blamed Spider-Man for his dad's death. As Peter was Spider-Man's photographer and friend, Harry also held him responsible.

**Harry of OsCorp** After his father died, Harry joined OsCorp Industries, and was put in charge of Special Projects. Despite this achievement, his hatred of Spider-Man, whom he called "The Bug," continued to eat away at him.

# CAUGHT IN
# A TANGLED WEB

They believed they were friends, but few friendships were ever tested so deeply as that between Peter Parker, M.J., and Harry Osborn. M.J. now knew Peter's secret heroic identity and had accepted it, but Peter himself seemed to have changed... or perhaps something had changed *him*. Adulation seemed to have gone to his head, making him arrogant and rude. There was also a new girl on the scene—Gwen Stacy. Harry, meanwhile, still carried a torch for M.J. and nursed longstanding grudges against Peter and Spider-Man.

**Lasting love** M.J. and Peter's relationship had grown and deepened, despite Peter's lifestyle choice of secret Super Hero. However, with success seemingly going to Peter's head, their love faced new challenges.

**Wall-climber** Rescuing policeman's daughter Gwen Stacy hugely increased Spider-Man's prestige in the city. Gwen was very impressed by Spider-Man—and strangely drawn to his friend Peter Parker, too.

**Stardust** M.J. dreamed that one day she would be a famous actress—but instead of swinging on a star she found herself singing in a bar!

**Watching and waiting** When M.J. landed a part in a Broadway show, Harry was there at the opening night. He was pleased for M.J., but deeply resentful of her relationship with Peter Parker.

**Mixed emotions** M.J. was shocked to discover that Peter and Gwen were lab partners. She wondered why Peter had never mentioned it.

**Bad vibes** Peter had decided to propose to M.J. at a swanky restaurant. However, M.J. stormed out and the ring stayed in his pocket.

**On the rebound** M.J.'s rift with Peter led to her drawing closer to her old flame, Harry Osborn.

**Heirloom** Aunt May gave Peter the engagement ring that Uncle Ben had given her. Would M.J. ever get to wear it?

# FLINT
# MARKO

Branded a criminal all his life, Flint Marko was always in the wrong place at the wrong time. Now he was on the run. Marko was determined that this time he would stay free: he would not be going back to jail. Marko had robbed and fought the law for no particular reason, but now he had a cause worth fighting for. His daughter's life was threatened by a mysterious disease. Only medical research could save her, and medical research cost money, lots of money.

**Social misfit** Marko saw himself as the victim of a world that had never shown him any kindness. He was willing to hit back against society if that meant saving the life of his daughter. If only he had the power...

**Signature look** Marko escaped jail in a laundry van. When it crashed, he stole a green and black T-shirt to blend in with the crowd and escape pursuing police.

**Criminal past** His ill daughter was the only person Flint Marko cared for. He was prepared to go to any lengths to save her life.

**Criminal past** Marko's former cellmate hinted that Marko could have been involved in a serious street crime, for which another criminal, who had died near the scene, had taken the rap.

# EDDIE
# BROCK

New York was a tough place to make a living—so thought freelance snapper Eddie Brock. He was desperate for a steady job, and J. Jonah Jameson, the cynical editor of the *Daily Bugle*, seemed ready to hand him one. But there was a catch: Brock had to get a picture that proved beyond doubt that Spider-Man was a menace to society. In addition, Brock had a rival for a full-time post at the paper, a rival named Peter Parker, who was determined to show that Spider-Man was a genuine hero of the people. Before long, Eddie Brock and Peter Parker were the worst of enemies.

**Journalistic principles**
Eddie Brock had started out in journalism with high ideals. But where had they got him? Nowhere! If a little bending of the truth was what it took to get ahead, then that was what he would do. Spider-Man had it coming, anyway.

**The photographer** For years Peter had dreamed of being a professional photographer, a prizewinning photojournalist risking life and limb in the thick of the action. Working freelance for the *Bugle* was all very well, but he wanted a full-time job so he could marry M.J.

**Defending his name**
Spider-Man had put up with a great deal of provocation from the press, and from the *Bugle* in particular. At least Peter Parker had been able to exercise some control over the public image of the web-crawler by posing for his own pictures. Buoyed by the extra confidence—some called it arrogance—his black suit gave him, Peter was determined that no freeloading snapper was going to blacken the name of Spider-Man.

**Gentleman of the press** The *Daily Bugle* had often been an outspoken critic of the exploits of the red and blue Spider-Man. When the city's favorite hero began to appear in a sinister-looking black outfit, the paper's chief headline writer, editor J. Jonah Jameson, saw even greater scare-story potential. Spider-Man had made him look a fool up to now, and no one made J. Jonah Jameson look a fool. If Parker couldn't get Jameson a picture that proved Spider-Man was a criminal, he'd find someone who could...

# ACKNOWLEDGMENTS

**Picture Credit**

The publisher would like to thank Getty Images: National Geographic
for their permission to reproduce their photograph on pp 44-45
(background) of Everybody Loves a Hero.


Dorling Kindersley and the writer would like to thank
James Hinton at Marvel UK for his assistance and advice
and Jana Haney at Marvel Entertainment, Inc.,
without whom this book would probably not exist!

DK